# FIRE
# BOMBERS

# Osprey Colour Series

# FIRE
## BOMBERS

## Philip Wallick

Published in 1987 by Osprey Publishing Limited
27A Floral Street, London WC2E 9DP
Member company of the George Philip Group

British Library Cataloguing in Publication Data

Wallick, Philip
    Fire bombers. — (Osprey colour series)
    1. Aeronautics in fire extinction
    I. Title
    628.9'25        TH9360

ISBN 0-85045-802-1

Editor Dennis Baldry
Additional photography David Oliver
Captions Bill Gunston
Designed by David Tarbutt
Printed in Hong Kong

**Front cover** PELICAN 21, a Canadair CL-215 of
the French *Sécurité Civile* releases its load of water
during the course of scooping and dropping
practice around the Etang du Berre off Marseilles,
which is conveniently located near the aircraft's
Marignane base. Canadair had sold 111 CL-215s
by January 1987, 58 of them in Europe, and the
*Sécurité Civile* is expected to be an early customer
for the new turboprop CL-215T version
[Courtesy David Oliver]

**Title pages** Fire bombing is hard work and
usually involves flying from dawn to dusk,
sometimes for days on end if a really big fire takes
hold. These venerable Flying Fortresses have
earned a welcome respite as the sun sets behind
them

**Right** An Aérospatiale SA.350 AStar of the East
Bay Regional Park Police based at Hayward,
California, test drops 108 US gallons of plain water
from the dangling Bambi Bucket. EAGLE 5, flown
by chief pilot Sgt Randy Parent, can respond
rapidly to snuff out brush fires in the National
Parks around the San Francisco area
[Oliver]

**Back cover** A pristine Douglas B-26C Invader
parked on a crowded ramp at Chico, California, in
the spring of 1975 prior to being fitted with a
purpose-built fire retardant tank in Aero Union's
conversion shop. During the latter stages of WW2
(and later in Korea and Vietnam as the On Mark
A-26A) the Invader attack bomber had an
outstanding combat record. In wartime trim
Tanker No 4 would have been fitted with
lead-ship navigational equipment and, quite
possibly, $H_2S$ panoramic radar. With a pair of 2000
horsepower Pratt & Whitney R-2800 Double
Wasps, the Invader had little trouble lifting 1000
US gallons of retardant. The aircraft in the
background are (left to right) C-119, PV-2
Harpoon, C-123 and another C-119

Trees, and the myriad of living creatures which they support, are treasures which mankind cannot afford to lose. Forests form a vital part of the Earth's life support system; and — if responsibly husbanded — they represent an almost infinitely renewable source of one of mankind's oldest and most versatile raw materials, used for everything from the D.H Mosquito to the paper these words are printed on. By their very nature forests tend to be found in generally inaccessible places. One clumsy camper can start a fire which, if left unchecked, could transform the surrounding landscape from glistening greenery to a smouldering mass of ugly charcoal.

Only firebombers have the speed, accuracy and flexibility to localize and defeat a blaze half-way up a mountainside, a task achieved by laying a barrier of retardant in the path of the fire. This kind of flying is demanding and inherently dangerous, and many pilots simply don't have what it takes to haul a fully-loaded DC-6 into a 'bombing' run along a blazing inferno with mountain peaks brushing the wingtips.

This Colour Series book is Philip Wallick's tribute to the 'stick-and-rudder' men who fly to the fires. He would like to thank Aero Union Corporation and the California Division of Forestry for their assistance during the preparation of FIRE BOMBERS. He is also grateful to David Oliver for providing the material on the French *Sécurité Civile*, and Bill Gunston for writing the captions.

Philip Wallick is a professional freelance photographer based at Chico in California. All of the photographs in FIRE BOMBERS were taken with Nikon cameras and lenses, loaded with Kodachrome 64.

**Right** Behind 'bombers' there has to be a massive backup of ground support. This is the end of a retardant tank at Chico Air Attack Base, California

# Contents

# Boeing B-17 Flying Fortress

The Boeing B-17 was the greatest and most famous of the early post-war former warbirds to serve in the tanker role. The red dye was added to the Phos-chek or Fire-trol water mix for high visibility, especially on the ground

A B-17 of Aero Union lets go its load of about
1800 US gallons on a fire at Paradise, California
(near the Chico Air Attack Base) in 1971. The only
evidence of the fire is the smoke on the right

**Above** Flying a B-17 needed strong muscles,
because this strategic bomber had tremendous
built-in stability. Once you were lined up there
was little you could do about it, and if a ground
fireman got in the way he sure got wet — with red
retardant

**Left** This B-17 was actually a rare Navy PB-1, seen awaiting conversion into a firefighting water bomber. Beyond is a B-25 Mitchell already converted to the tanker role. Except in California, the B-25 Mitchell saw much service as a firebomber, carrying 1000 US gallons

**Top left** Front end of one of a very large number of B-17 firebomber tankers. While the wartime exploits of the famous Fortress have filled dozens of published books, not much has been written about the type's post-war tanker role; but individual B-17s flew more hours as tankers than they did as bombers!

**Above** The firebomber B-17s converted with many kinds of locally contrived modification to replace the wartime turrets, the most noticeable differences being in the nose. Ship 19, seen operating with Aero Union from Chester, California, was one of the ones with a pointed aluminium nose. Pilot and copilot normally got aboard through the open door, reaching up with both arms and swinging their legs up and inside

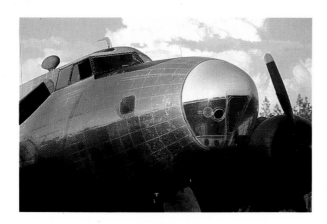

**Above** This B-17 ended up with a moulded Plexiglas nose reminiscent of the wartime B-17F. Virtually all the air tanker B-17s had been B-17Gs, and in the conversion had gained totally new nose sections, as well as major modifications elsewhere

**Right** Air Tanker No 09, seen at Chester, California, as late as 1976, was one of those with a metal nose which followed the contours of the original, even to the extent of having a 'bombardier' panel. The slightly bulged belly tank, occupying the lower part of the former bomb bay, can just be seen. It was common to start a day hauling 1600 US gallons and switch to 1800 if all went well

**Below** During the summer fire season the days were so busy that maintenance had to be done at night. The four slits behind each engine are cooling air exits. The ghostly shape under the wing is caused by ground crew moving around during the long time-exposure, carrying a torch

**Preceding pages** Starting engines at Redding, California, in 1976. The Fort was universally liked, being generally regarded as flying like an enlarged Piper Cub; but its rock-like stability was a problem near the fire

**Left** Bill Waldman in the left seat of Tanker No 17 of Aero Union. Everyone liked having a copilot, especially a copilot who could do the mundane chores of washing, oiling and endlessly checking such things as the retardant load and centre of gravity position. Takeoff was a two-man job, the non-flying pilot reading out manifold pressure and airspeed and working the gear and flaps

**Right** Port pair of R-1820 Cyclones en route to the fire. The engines retained their GE turbosuper-chargers, making for excellent performance under high-altitude conditions. The propellers were 11-ft 7-in Hamilton Standards

Aero Union No 17 about to touch down at Chester, California. With its totally manual controls, the B-17 had to be manoeuvred with muscle power, though in turns it had an odd tendency to overbank and sometimes the pilot in desperation would close down the engines on the high wing to try to bring it down. Near the airfield it was difficult to lose speed until the ASI had fallen to the flap limit of 142 mph

Tanker 17 landing at Chester for a reload in 1975.
The dust clearly shows the aerodynamics of the
wings, which are still creating lift and tip vortices.
To modern pilots this big taildragger posed
unexpected problems in its tendency to swing
(swap ends on takeoff or landing). With a
crosswind the pilot really had to earn his pay

Tails of fire bombers awaiting call at Chico. All had the so-called Cheyenne tail turret, introduced with the final production batches (B-17G-90-BO, -50-DL and -55-VE), which reduced overall length by 5 inches. Ship 18 retains the gunner's transparent panels. In the background, an S-2 Tracker

Tail-on view of Chico fire-bomber No 19, whose aluminium skin over the former tail gunner's position warns 'Full when light goes out'. Today this particular B-17 has been as far as possible restored to wartime standard and is on display at Castle Air Force Base Museum, California

**Overleaf** Aero Union No 19 parked at sunset in 1971, with No 1 propeller feathered. This particular fire bomber looked more like a transport than a bomber, resembling the C-108, CB-17 and local transport rebuilds in Sweden and Indo-China. The streamlining made no significant difference to fire-bomber performance

Major maintenance in the Aero Union hangar at Chico in preparation for the 1975 season. This particular B-17 has a streamlined nose but retains the projecting balconies for the hand-aimed cheek guns, which were added along with the chin turret to provide the greatest possible firepower against head-on attack

Another view of maintenance before the start of
the 1975 season. The bomb doors are open, as they
are in most fire-bomber conversions during release
of retardant

The handsomely finished Black Hills No 89: in the background is the Aero Union hangar at Chester, California, and between the main gears can be glimpsed part of the fire-retardant tank farm.

**Above** No 89 starting engines before a firefighting mission. The row of retardant storage tanks can be seen in the background, together with the landing gears of a DC-6, a considerably more powerful tanker able to put down a heavier load

Strikingly painted in white, red and black, a B-17 of Black Hills Aviation, whose home base is Alamagordo, New Mexico. From this angle the projecting bay doors under the retardant tank can be seen clearly. Normal payload is 1600 US gallons

Thirty inches manifold...airborne, gear up. Black
Hills No 89 gets airborne at Chester in the hot
summer of 1976. The B-17 was always popular,
but with 1800 gallons pilots normally felt they had
a choice of climbing straight ahead or making a
turn and losing height, but not of turning and
climbing at the same time

**Left** A 1984 picture taken at Mesa, Arizona, showing one of the last B-17s to remain active, almost 50 years after the B-17's first flight at Seattle and 40 years after the first flight of this particular example. Throughout, the old bomber's structure never gave a moment's real worry. The worst problems, to a pilot familiar with the type, was its rock-like stability

**Above** The last bomber, parked in the sunshine at Mesa. Note the remarkable array of avionics antennas, and the stencilled 'MAX LD 16250 LBS, 1805 GALS'

**Left** End of a once proud bomber: a B-17 of Aero Union whose inability to make sharp manoeuvres brought it to grief whilst fighting a fire in the early 1970s. It had been tanker No 16 of Aero Union

**Above** Another bomber of Aero Union that bit the California dust — having probably survived flak and fighters more than 30 years previously. Also seen in the next illustration, this aircraft had the legend 'EMPTY WT 32,633' stencilled below the cockpit on the left side

**Overleaf** Another view of Aero Union No 18 after coming to grief, but without giving its crew more than a shaking. Considering the enormous total of hours flown by the B-17 tankers the accident record was commendable

# Canadair CL-215

Canadair's CL-215 represents a totally new breed of aircraft, actually designed as a firefighting waterbomber. Instead of having to return to the airport for a reload, it can scoop up plain water as it skims across a lake or sea — if necessary with six-foot waves. A Yugoslav CL-215 made 225 drops in a single day, putting down 317,540 US gallons! This is a French example based at Marseilles Marignane airport
[Oliver]

**Above** Firefighting pilots around the world are normally experienced as pilots, and incidentally the last repository of practical handling experience with big piston engines. This is *Sécurité Civile* pilot Hubert Bolzinger, ex-*Aéronavale*, with a wealth of experience on Lancaster, Neptune, Crusader and Etendard aircraft
[Oliver]

**Left** This CL-215 is one of the yellow fleet of 16 delivered to France's *Sécurité Civile*, seen parked at Marignane. Powered by two 2100 horsepower R-2800 Double Wasps, the plank-winged Canadair is an amphibian, with retractable tricycle landing gear
[Oliver]

**Above** Close-up of a *Sécurité Civile* CL-215. Tests in France and Spain have demonstrated the effectiveness against forest fires of scooping up fresh or salt water and mixing it on board automatically with a suitable foaming agent stored in an aircraft tank
[Oliver]

**Overleaf** Adjacent to Marignane are the mighty waters of the Etang de Berre, from which the CL-215s can operate with gear retracted. Here one gets 'on the step'. Weights for water operation are lower than from a runway, but takeoff run is about 2600 feet in either case
[Oliver]

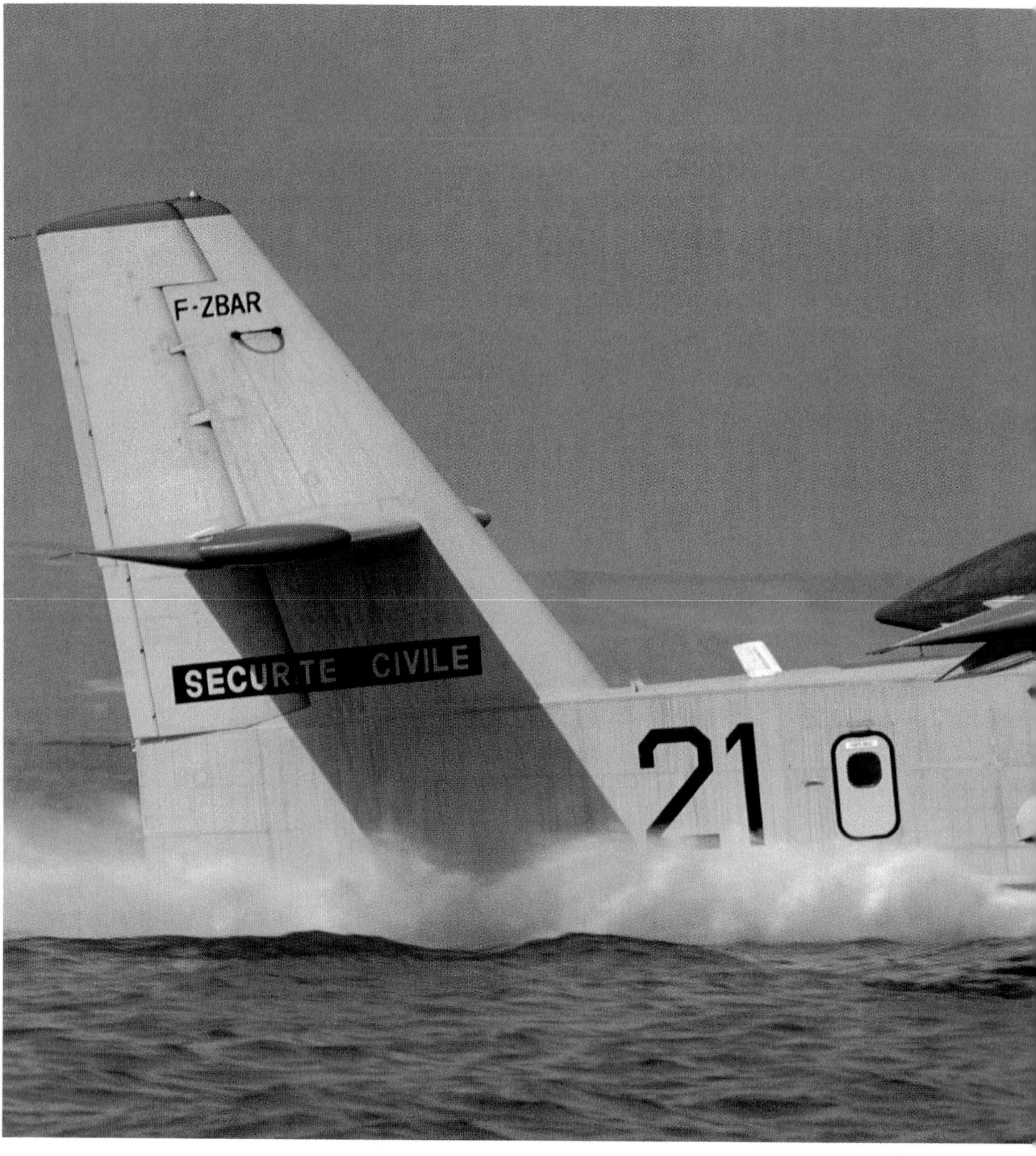
F-ZBAR
SECURITE CIVILE
21

Taxying on the Etang de Berre with engines idling.
Note the thick high-lift wing profile chosen to
match the needs of a firefighting waterbomber. At
maximum landing weight the power-off stalling
speed is only 76 mph
[Oliver]

This CL-215, Canadian C-GMAF, suffered a landing gear problem when approaching Chico, California. The main wheels moved out from their recesses but failed to extend further, so the pilot put the aircraft down in a field near the airport

**Overleaf** C-GMAF left only shallow grooves in the field, and itself suffered very little damage and was soon flying again. The relatively small size of the fuselage reflects the high density of water, compared with other types of payload. There are two tanks, each with its own pickup scoop, dump door and control system, totalling 1411 US gallons, or 12,000 lb. Though it has a modest fuselage, or hull, the CL-215 has a giant tail for good control at low airspeeds. Compared with the old converted warbirds the Canadian amphibian is orders of magnitude more efficient and effective, but of course its purchase price reflects 1980s manufacture. Today Canadair is building an advanced turboprop version, the CL-215T, powered by Pratt & Whitney Canada PW100s

45

# Consolidated Privateer

Remarkably few B-24 Liberators ever served as firefighting bombers. This very unusual variant was formerly a P4Y-2G of the US Coast Guard, rebuilt with circular (instead of vertical ellipse) engine cowls, housing Wright R-2600 engines of 1700 horsepower from B-25s, and with many other changes. The observer nose was peculiar to this rare Coast Guard model. **Above** Another view of the converted P4Y-2G, which itself was a much-modified derivative of the Navy PB4Y-2 Privateer, which in turn was a gross redesign of a late-model B-24. This view shows well the engine installation, which bears no relation to anything originally fitted to any P4Y-2G, PB4Y-2 or B-24! Note the steps up the side of the fuselage

49

**Above** Cockpit of the P4Y-2G, with a bonedome resting on the left control-wheel shaft. In World War 2 the Liberator family were second only to the B-29 as being the most complex and demanding production aircraft

**Right** The tail of the P4Y-2G is broadly similar to that of the PB4Y-2 Privateer, apart from having no turret and greatly enlarged side observer stations (the Privateer had smaller projecting blisters, which originally carried guns). The tail was similar to that of the Liberator C.IX and RY-3, but not the same as that of the final production bomber, the B-24N

**Left** A room with a view: the gaint waist observer windows of the former Coast Guard aircraft almost made one wonder what was holding the tail on. This view is looking forward, past what in other versions would have been the bomb bay and on to the cockpit

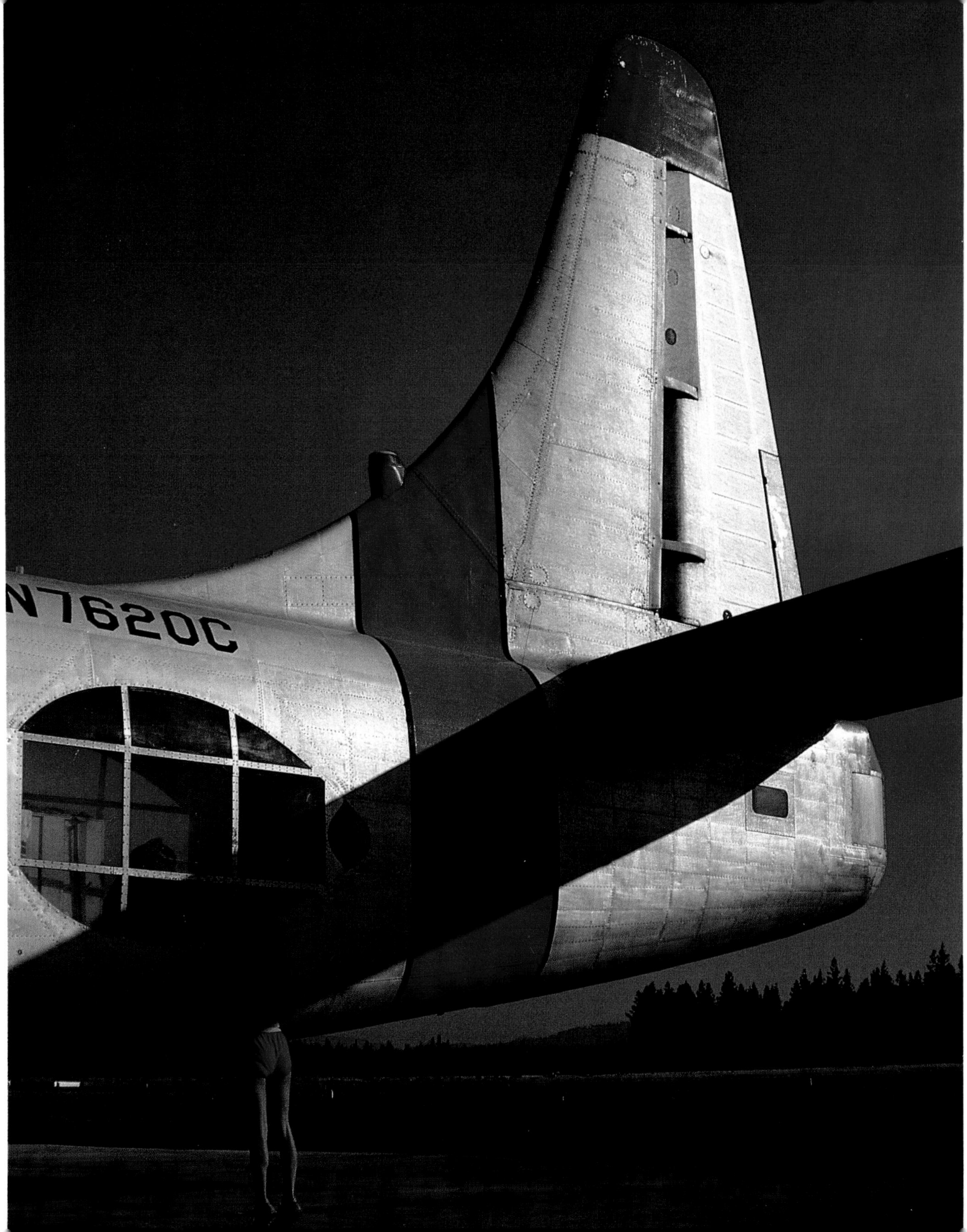
N7620C

Just getting airborne at Chester is the last surviving operational PB4Y-2 Privateer, which like the P4Y-2G previously described originally stemmed from the B-24 Liberator programme. Also like the former Coast Guard aircraft, this Privateer has been rebuilt with much more powerful B-25 engines in circular engine cowlings

Here the surviving PB4Y-2 (operated by Hawkins
and Powers) is just beginning to tuck away its
gear, the giant single wheels swinging out and up to
lie in recesses in the thin wings. All the single-fin
members of the family not only had better control
than the mass produced twin-fin aircraft but also
had reduced drag. The PB4Y also had dihedral on
the tailplane (horizontal stabilizer)

**Overleaf** Gear fast disappearing as the PB4Y
leaves Chester's runway astern. Despite high
weights and a much higher wing loading the PB4Y
had better climb than the B-17 and was
considerable more manoeuvrable

The PB4Y was first used in the firebomber role in 1959. It could carry 2000 US gallons, and dump it all on a fire at once. This was the first time anything like this kind of knock-out blow had been possible. A little earlier, during tests at Ramona, in Southern California, a YC-97 had been used with 4000-gallon capacity, but it could only put down 1000 gallons at a time

**Right** As in the previous picture the PB4Y-2 here has takeoff flap selected, but the gear is fully retracted. Unlike the B-24 bombers these aircraft never had turbosuperchargers, since high-altitude

performance was unimportant. This aircraft has the nose of an early B-24D or PB4Y-1 spliced on, replacing the PB4Y-2's bulbous gun turret

**Overleaf** Touching down at Chester, the PB4Y-2 shows in side view the oil coolers hung under the rear of each engine nacelle. In the original aircraft the oil radiators were tucked away in ducts inside the deep vertical-ellipse cowlings. The life of a firebomber is hard, operating consistently at high power in hot summer air at low level — to say nothing of flying through the fire!

# Big Dougs

**Left** Among the happier firebomber conversions have been the Douglas Commercials, though these have tended initially to cost rather more than surplus bombers. Here, in fully operational trim, Aero Union DC-4 No 2 gets away from Chester in the late 1970s

Aero Union's Tanker 16 is a DC-4 which was painted in Bicentennial livery for the 1776-1976 celebrations at Chester. It was photographed still in the proud livery seven years later — during the rainy season, when its services would not be called upon

Powered by R-2800 Double Wasp engines, and with a pressurized fuselage, the DC-6 was instantly distinguishable from the wartime DC-4 by its square passenger windows. Here an American Airlines DC-6 still wears its old livery whilst waiting for conversion to its new role

Pictured prior to conversion, this aircraft is a real oddball: an ex-Navy R5D (R5D-2 if the modex on the nose is the last three digits of its BuNo), it was clearly used for special research, and bristles with modifications

Takeoff by a DC-4 from Chester, on the power of
its 1350-horsepower R-2000 engines, a slightly
enlarged version of the familiar Pratt & Whitney
Twin Wasp. Even at this point the pilot could still
see the photographer, through the big and flat
front windshield

**Overleaf** Fly-by by DC-4 No 18 of Aero Union, with civil registration N4218S. Several of the DC-4s had actually been C-54s and VC-54s of the Air Force, several actually seeing service on the Berlin Airlift in 1948-49

**Following pages** This DC-6 is one of the more stylishly painted tankers. Operating from Chico, California, it serves along with a fleet of other types including the Neptune parked to the rear. These great Douglases have paddle-blade propellers turned by 2500-horsepower Double Wasps, which make light work of a 3000-gallon load

Another Aero Union DC-4 comes in to land. As might be expected these aircraft posed no significant problems in performance or handling. The only drawback to using such aircraft is that they have to come back for a reload, and this takes time, needs a hustling ground crew and strains the aircraft in the landing and takeoff

**Above** Ground checkout of the retardant installation in a firefighting DC-6, using plain water. The belly tank added to these aircraft usually has a capacity of 3000 US gallons, but this example belongs to the *Sécurité Civile* in France and is calibrated in litres. A 3000 US gallon load, ignoring the tank and installation, represents a dead weight of 25,000 lb

**Left** Nose of the Chico DC-6, showing the anti-dazzle black panel which is found on virtually all water bombers to make it easier to look ahead over the nose in brilliant sunshine. The pointed nose shows that radar was fitted, and this — usually unlike the pressurization system — invariably is maintained in operative condition

**Below and inset** The water container is entirely external to the pressurized fuselage, being slung beneath in a way that avoids the tank having to carry any inflight loads other than the evenly distributed mass of water. Internal baffles cut down sloshing. On pilot command the entire load can be dumped by opening flaps along each side over the full length. This avoids any change in longitudinal trim as the water leaves, which at low level could be dangerous

Gear up and an Aero Union DC-4 gets away from Chester. Note the crosswind, which has carried the aircraft well away from the runway centreline despite crabbing the aircraft round into wind. This would have posed real problems with a B-17 and several other 'bombers'

Operating on this occasion out of Chico, a DC-4 of
Aero Union banks steeply over the fire before
letting go its 2000-gallon load over the best spot.
While a good pilot can always put the retardant
down directly on the fire itself, in four missions
out of five the task is instead to lay an
impenetrable trail of retardant in the fire's path

Though neither an air force nor an airline, France's *Sécurité Civile* nevertheless is proud of its triangle-in-circle insignia. Here it adorns a beautifully prepared DC-6B, seen at Marseilles Marignane. The starboard R-2800s are running, and No 2 is just beginning to turn over [Oliver]

Filling both the left and right tanks of DC-6B No
61 with 11,500 litres of water. This is equivalent to
2530 Imperial gallons, or 3036 US gallons. The
mass varies slightly depending on whether fresh or
salt water is used, and whether a foaming additive
is employed
[Oliver]

This DC-6B of the *Sécurité Civile* has a different tank installation, similar to that on the DC-6B photographed at Chico (Pages 68-71). It also retains all its passenger windows, and can be used as a general utility transport, especially during the winter
[Oliver]

**Right** Most powerful of all the piston-engined Douglas Commercials, the DC-7 still carries the same 3000 US gallon load as the DC-6. This example is doing a test drop with plain water at Chico in 1975. Over a fire it would probably get down to rather lower altitude, if the terrain permitted

Assisted by a ground power truck a DC-7 starts its
3250-horsepower Wright R-3350
Turbo-Compound engines, which though massive
and expensive offered unprecedented power and
fuel economy. The pilot may be checking flap
operation; full landing flap has been selected

The starboard Turbo-Compounds of a DC-7 tanker running up on the ramp. Unlike earlier DC airliners the DC-7 has four-blade propellers, in this case by Hamilton Standard. Originally only the super long-range DC-7C version had spinners

**Right** A DC-7C Seven Seas tanker about to taxi out. Douglas achieved such a pinnacle of aerodynamic refinement with the 7C that its drag was the same as that of a rod stretched between the wing tips with a diameter of *one inch*!

Half-way house: originally in scheduled service with an airline, this DC-7 was one of several operated by Ports of Call, a Denver charter company, before being converted as a firebomber in the 1970s. By chance, back in 1953 Douglas Aircraft was engaged in testing the prototype DC-7 and used water as ballast. When the load was dumped through a 6-inch pipe it was found it wetted the ground, and special tests took place at Arcadia and Palmdale. But in those days the $1,600,000 flagship was totally uneconomic as a firefighter; 20 years of depreciation did the trick, however

The essential stepladder is pulled on board a DC-7C of Aero Union. The ultimate piston-engined DC, the famed Seven Seas was a happy result of adding 5 feet to each wing centre section. This gave more lift, made room for more fuel and moved the propellers away from the fuselage so that not even 3400-horsepower Turbo-Compounds caused quite such a racket and vibration inside the cabin.

**Right** About to reach terra firma from the lofty elevation of a Seven Seas. Costly to maintain and operate, the Seven Seas was designed to fly the North Atlantic non-stop, and what is really needed is some way of putting its enormous internal fuel capacity to work with fire retardant instead of 115/145-grade gasoline. In firefighting a typical mission radius is more like 40 miles rather than 4000

# Fairchild Flying Boxcar and Provider

**Left** In fact there are only five C-119s present, but the tail booms tend to multiply the numbers. With the jet booster these were not bad aircraft, but they suffered from one slight handicap: the wings tended to fall off. This slightly bothered the pilots, who eventually considered it might be preferable if they picked a different kind of tanker. In fairness to Fairchild, the original design never envisaged intensive flying with massive loads at ground level, pulling plenty of G through some of the bumpiest air (you get quite a thermal over a forest fire)

This beautifully painted Dollar-Nineteen has the Steward-Davis jet booster pack on top, housing a Westinghouse J34 putting out 3400 lb of thrust to help along the two R-2800 Double Wasps. One tanker driver, operating out of Boise, Idaho, said 'Man, with 2400 gallons on board if we could get a positive rate of climb of 150 feet per minute off the runway that was spectacular. With the jet we could get 1000'

Like the preceding aircraft this C-119 belongs to the great fleet of Aero Union, and it is thundering out of Chico, California. With brilliant rate of roll and spring-tab elevators there was no problem in control (to an experienced pilot, who, for example, would avoid aileron stalls at even 170 knots), but on landing the ineffective flaps were rated as terrible

**Below** Beyond the fire-retardant loading hose are Fairchild C-119 Flying Boxcars, retired after honourable service with the US Air Force and converted into tankers. Always known as the Dollar-nineteen, they were generally regarded as surprisingly agile but underpowered

Aero Union tanker No 63 was another Fairchild, a C-123 Provider. Originally developed by Chase Aircraft during the Korean war, the C-123 was in the class of the C-119 and had similar R-2800 engines, but in general it was lighter and more efficient. It was especially good as the C-123K with underwing jet booster pods (General Electric J85s of 2850 lb thrust each), as fitted here, which made it almost sprightly

**Overleaf** Beyond the Aero Union C-123K a company DC-4 makes a steep approach after a summer mission. The scene looks beautiful; but one has to remember that it is to preserve such scenery that the tankers fly their hazardous missions. Incidentally, the C-123 was one of the tankers whose retardant installation ended in flush belly doors. When the load of red-dyed liquid gushed forth it stained the belly all the way back to the tip of the tailcone

87

# Grumman greats

**Left** Of all the early firebombers none was greater than the great Grumman 'Turkey'. The original model was Grumman's TBF, but in fact the biggest production comprised TBMs made by Eastern Aircraft Division of General Motors, and today most of the tankers are called TBMs. This view of a TBM starting its Wright R-2600 Cyclone at Mesa, Arizona, emphasizes the giant spread of wing

Designed as a wartime carrier-based torpedo bomber, the Grumman Avenger (TBF or TBM) was one of the great war-winners. When young it was judged almost faultless, but when they were the backbone of the California State firefighting contract in 1958-73 the TBMs were old, and no two flew alike — one would appear to have power-boosted controls while another had controls seemingly set in cement. At best it was a two-hands aircraft, and if you had the wrong rudder trim on takeoff no human leg ever made could save you!

The cockpit of a retired TBM parked at Mesa. This aircraft has already lost several cockpit items, but it retains a radar display screen (though of course the radar would be removed during conversion for the air tanker role). These venerable machines were enjoyable to fly, if you had good muscles, but were withdrawn around 1972 when it was decided all tankers had to be multi-engined

**Left** Back in 1954 famed Hollywood pilot Paul Mantz and Cod Jensen pioneered the use of the Avenger as a firebomber, using a 600 US gallon plywood tank. Here in 1977, at Cod Jensen's field, a TBM rests in honourable retirement, showing the much later multi-door tank which released liquid from separate cells in succession

The original TBF was the first aircraft ever designed from the start with Leroy Grumman's patented 'Sto-Wing' which pivoted the wings back on skewed axes. Here old firebomber No 89 waits at Grass Valley in 1972 for Frank Ponti to come and restore it — which he did

**Right** Looking tired after its labours, a Globe Air TBM rests at Mesa, Arizona. In the 1950s and 1960s the various Avengers, mostly TBM-3s, were the most widely used firebombers in many Western states. It was at this time that sodium or calcium borate was commonly added to the water, in a concentration of four or five pounds per US gallon. This gave rise to the common term 'borate bomber'

Righting a much-modified TBM, which nosed over on the runway. The Avenger may have been a heavy aircraft to handle at all speeds, but it had no vices and nosing-over like this was uncommon. Note the wingtip endplates, a local modification

**Overleaf** The Grumman F7F Tigercat got into action just as World War 2 was drawing to a close, and because of its size, power and performance went to the Marines rather than to carrier-based squadrons. With two 2100-horsepower Double Wasps it was a truly awesome beast, and the hottest air tanker of all time — yet the average price paid prior to conversion as air tankers was around $1200!

**Left** With such power available the tanker operators had no hesitation in installing a mighty tank holding 1000 US gallons (though later 800 became more common). Making its run at a speed typically around 260 mph the F7F could really *attack* the fire. Manoeuvrability was excellent; it was hard to believe that the F7F, which weighed far more than a loaded Avenger, came from the same stable

An F7F tanker of Sis-Q Flying Services on final approach. Undoubtedly the only problem with these great aircraft was that they had to be flown all the time. When Phil Wallick interviewed F7F pilots one said 'That airplane was always ready to eat my lunch', and the other said 'If you weren't paying attention it would do something that would get your attention real sudden'!

Grumman's AF-2 Guardian was essentially 'Son of Avenger'. It saw Navy service as a hunter/killer team in the anti-submarine role, the AF-2W being packed with sensors for finding submarines and its partner AF-2S carrying the weapons. It was a typically sound Grumman product, but with a span exceeding 60 feet it really needed 3000 horsepower instead of a hardworked R-2800 Double Wasp putting out just 2400 on takeoff

**Bottom left** Once an AF-2S anti-submarine attack aircraft, N99957 became Aero Union No 21, a rare firebomber tanker. Visibility was superb, but the climbout was slow and flat, and pushing the stick sideways produced little roll response until eventually the roll spoilers came into action. A spin would have been lethal

Guardian No 21 making a drop of red Fire-trol retardant in the path of a fire. Capacity was 800 US gallons, a load of about 8400 lb. The cockpit seated two side-by-side but in the air tanker role there was no need for a second crew member

**Overleaf** Derelict AF-2 Guardians left at Chico, California, with a Howard or Learstar conversion of the Lockheed Lodestar at the far end. Grumman aircraft are always called 'products of the Iron Works', because of their unbreakable strength. Like old soldiers they just fade away, typically in lineups such as this

Stripped of most items of value, this former AF-2S still has its 800-gallon retardant tank, occupying the former weapon bay. For the record, the AF-2 was the production version of the XTB3F-1, which had the same Double Wasp in the nose but also had a Westinghouse turbojet in the tail, fed by inlets in the wing roots. It was judged that the booster turbojet was not worth having, but maybe the later air tanker drivers would have disagreed!

104

Another derelict AF-2S in the firebomber air
tanker boneyard at Chico. The wings folded in the
same way as those of the Avenger, upper surface
facing outward. The slat can be seen, as well as the
bay which housed the retracted main gear. Note
also the auxiliary fins, and the rudder which was
hydraulically boosted to overcome the otherwise
severe problem of propeller torque on takeoff

This AF-2S never got to become an air tanker, but still rests in its original Navy Reserve livery, from Akron, Ohio. The cable can be seen which restrained the folded wings from any movement in a high wind

After retirement from the air tanker industry this Guardian was reconverted back to AF-2S standard and beautifully restored to flying condition as an exhibit at the US Naval Air Museum at Pensacola, Florida. Another restored Guardian survives in flying condition at Oshkosh, Wisconsin, home of the Experimental Aircraft Association

Front end of yet another firebombing Grumman,
an S-2 Tracker. Though it only has about the same
horsepower as an AF-2 Guardian the S-2 managed
to combine both the anti-submarine hunter and
killer roles in the one aircraft. As a firefighting
tanker it was definitely superior. Engines were
1525-horsepower Wright R-1820 Cyclones,
advanced versions of the same engine as used in
the B-17

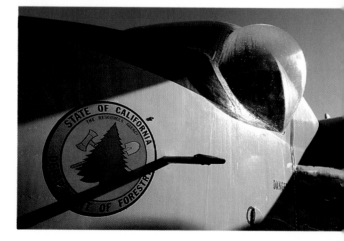

**Left** The California Department of Forestry S-2A sported amazing bugeye observation blisters on each side of the cockpit. Thanks to this all-round vision, their excellent agility and long endurance, the S-2 was often used by the two key people in air attack, the Air Attack Supervisor, who stands off with a high overview of the whole situation, and the ATCO, Air Tanker Co-Ordinator, who takes part in the fight but also deploys aircraft to the best advantage

Tail view of California State tanker No 78, showing the double-hinged rudder giving very powerful control even at low airspeeds. In the air tanker role the usual load of retardant is 800 US gallons. Nothing was put in the rear part of the engine nacelles, which in Navy service housed the anti-submarine sonobuoys which were shot out to the rear

CDF (California Department of Forestry) S-2 tankers parked at Chico Air Attack Base, along with the oldest Cyclone-engined tankers, the B-17s of Aero Union. Thanks to the sheer size and complexity of the US accessory industry, spare parts for R-1820 engines, and countless other items, are still readily available

**Below** Even on the ground things sometimes don't go quite according to plan. Here at Chico Air Attack Base in 1983 a faulty valve in the retardant loading hose disconnects from the S-2 and instead of filling the tank sprays the pristine aircraft a dirty red. On this occasion the trip had to be abandoned, and the pilot — who gets paid by results — switched everything off, climbed out and had a few words to say to the unhappy loading crew. Guess who had to scrub down the aircraft!

Certainly the best S-2 air tanker conversions are those marketed by Conair Aviation of Abbotsford, British Columbia, Canada. The Conair Firecat is a total rebuild and update, with an 870 US gallon tank divided into four compartments and with optional microchip control. Among many other changes are a raised cabin floor, big low-pressure tyres and a new cockpit. This one belongs to France's *Sécurité Civile*, which has ten of these efficient aircraft based at Marseilles Marignane [Oliver]

# Lockheed Neptune

**Left** The Lockheed P-2 Neptune is one of the biggest and most powerful of the twin-engined tankers. Indeed, some might be considered four-engined, because they have jet booster pods, but these are not fitted to this example, which appears in the next six illustrations

The P-2H cockpit was, like the aircraft itself, rather cosy for extremely long ocean patrons, though a tall pilot could stretch his legs. As a tanker the P-2 can be flown solo, though workload is rather higher than with most other types

Though it was first flown as long ago as 1954, the final model of Neptune, at first called the P2V-7 and after 1962 the P-2H (or SP-2H in anti-submarine form), served in front-line Navy squadrons until 1966, and went on much longer with the Reserves. One of its features was this completely new cockpit giving good all-round visibility

**Left** Beautifully painted in Aero Union livery, P-2H Tanker 01 was still not fully converted when these photographs were taken, and (as the gap in the former weapon bay shows) the retardant tank had not then been fitted. The big and powerful P-2 can take a 3000-US gallon load. This one has a new metal nose

Main engines of the P-2H are two Wright R-3350-32W Turbo-Compounds, each rated at 3500 horsepower, turning four-blade Hamilton Standard Hydromatic propellers of 15-ft 2-in diameter. This combination easily coped with a gross weight exceeding 76,000 lb, in the P-2E version, considerably heavier than any B-17!

The P-2 was one of the first aircraft to be fitted with MAD (magnetic anomaly detection) gear, which finds submarines by detecting distortion caused to the Earth's magnetic field. The sensor had to be as far as possible from the disturbance caused by the aircraft itself, so it was put at the tip of a very long tail extension. It was left on Tanker 01, but many tanker P-2s had the tail cut short

**Overleaf** An overall view of Tanker 01 awaiting its new tank on the Aero Union ramp. The Fowler flaps are lowered, but the newly converted Neptune still looks sleek and capable. P-2s began to fight fires in 1969, and substantial numbers serve in Oregon. It will probably be many years before something with turbine engines can come along and do a better job

Parked on the same ramp as the Aero Union P-2 Tanker 01, this P-2H belongs to another operator, Evergreen Air Tankers, which operates from Missoula in the state of Montana (which is almost as big as California). In this head-on shot the P-2's jet pods stand out well. Each contains a Westinghouse J34 turbojet of 3400 lb thrust. They permit operation at increased weight and make a big difference to takeoff and initial climb. The aircraft was converted at the Evergreen Air Center, part of the Marana Air Park complex in Arizona

This Evergreen P-2 has the operator's handsome
white livery with green cheatline. It also retains
the original transparent nose, but (like most other
P-2 tankers) it has lost its original wingtip fuel
tanks

In this view the P-2H's jet pods are clearly seen, as is the capacious payload tank — one of the biggest in current use. The P-2 is not a cheap aircraft to maintain, but it is one of the best firebomber tankers so far to become available

The P-2's span of 103 ft 10 in in its original form is actually slightly greater than the span of a B-17, but the high aspect-ratio wing has considerably less area. Note the 'sawn off' tail, where the MAD stinger used to be. Sadly, the market could not support a totally new purpose-designed tanker, other than the Canadair CL-215, so conversions are likely to rule the Western states for the rest of the century

**Overleaf** The predecessor of the P-2 Neptune on the Lockheed production line was the wartime PV-2 Harpoon. It was hardly in the same class, being a kind of grandson of the pre-war Lodestar transport with two R-2800 Double Wasp engines and a bigger wing. In the air tanker role it carried 1000 US gallons, as did such broadly similar wartime twins as the B-25 Mitchell and B-26 Invader. All these have now been pensioned off

Going back to the early days of aerial firefighting, following inconclusive tests with such types as the P-47, AD-2 and even the B-29 (!) the first practical Air Attack Squadron was formed at Mendocino, California, in 1956, equipped with light trainer biplanes such as the N3N Canary and PT-75

Kaydet! They proved the basic techniques but with a miniscule 180 gallons at a time. Today Ag-planes are getting back into the act, and in 1986 the Ag-Cat began fighting fires. Designed by Grumman and built by Schweizer, this B-model Ag-Cat is making a test drop with plain water